SHIRLEY VALENTINE

A play by

WILLY RUSSELL

Samuel French – London
New York – Sydney – Toronto – Hollywood

SHIRLEY VALENTINE

Inside Mrs Joe Bradshaw — 42 year-old mother of two grown children — is the former Shirley Valentine longing to get out. Her hope and self-confidence badly shattered by school, marriage and life, she is reduced to talking to the kitchen wall whilst preparing her husband's evening meal — to be on the table as he opens the front door every night. As she sips a glass of wine she dreams of drinking in a country where the grape is grown. Her feminist friend offers her a holiday in Greece and, with great trepidation and a lot of forward planning, Shirley seizes the opportunity and goes, to encounter a totally different lifestyle. Shirley, breaking out of the mould cast for her by society, is brilliantly shown with humour, warm sympathy and human insight by the author of *Educating Rita* and *Blood Brothers*.

SHIRLEY VALENTINE

First presented in London by Bob Swash at the Vaudeville Theatre on 21st January, 1988, with the following cast:

Shirley	Pauline Collins

Directed by Simon Callow
Designed by Bruno Santini

SYNOPSIS OF SCENES

ACT I, SCENE 1 The kitchen of a semi-detached house. Evening
ACT I, SCENE 2 The same. Three weeks later

ACT II A Greek island

ACT I

Scene 1

The kitchen of a semi-detached house. It is a well established kitchen, bearing signs of additions and alterations which have been made over the years . It is not a highly personalized palace of pitch pine and hanging baskets but nevertheless has signs of personality having overcome the bleakness of chipboard and formica. It is quite a comfortable and reassuring place

Specifically the kitchen contains — apart from the obvious cooker, fridge etc. — a door which leads out of the house, a wall with a window, a dining-table and chairs

As the CURTAIN *rises Shirley is beginning preparations for cooking the evening meal — this includes opening a bottle of white wine from which she pours a glass. Throughout the following scene she sets a table for two, as she prepares, cooks and finally serves one of the truly great but unsung dishes of world cuisine— chips and egg*

SHIRLEY
Y'know I like a glass of wine when I'm doin' the cookin'. Don't I, wall? Don't I like a glass of wine when I'm preparing the evenin' meal? Chips an' egg!

She takes a sip of wine

I never used to drink wine. It was our Millandra who started me on this. She said to me, she said, "Mother! Mother, nobody drinks rum an' coke these days. Everybody drinks wine now." Kids. They know everything, don't they? Our Millandra was goin' through her slightly intellectual phase at the time. Y'know her, an' her mate — Sharron-Louise. Because it was all white wine an' Bruce

Springsteen at the time. Y' know the pair of them stopped goin' down the clubs in town an' started hangin' out in that bistro all the time. Y' know, where the artists go. They seen, erm, what's-his-name one night, erm, Henry Adrian, yeh. Apparently Sharron-Louise got his autograph. And breakfast as well, I believe. Anyway, the pair of them are out of that phase now. And am I glad. Because y' know the two of them'd sit at the table for hours an' all's you'd hear from the pair of them was — "It was great. It was great. Was a laugh, wasn't it?" Then they'd both go back into trance for half an hour an' you'd suddenly hear — "It was brilliant last night. It was more than brilliant. It was mega brill." "Yeh, it was, it was double fab, wasn't it?" And d' y' know, no matter how long they sat there, you'd never get to know what it was that was double fab an' mega brill.

Pause

Maybe it was the breakfasts! Mind you, I do miss them, the kids. Our Millandra shares a flat with Sharron-Louise now. An' our Brian's livin' in a squat. In Kirkby. I said to him, I said, "Brian, if you're gonna live in a squat, son, couldn't y' pick somewhere nice. Y' know, somewhere like Childwall?" "Mother," he said to me, "Childwall is no place for a poet." 'Cos that's our Brian's latest scheme, y' see. He's always got a scheme. This one is — he's become Britain's first-ever busker poet. What's he like, wall? The language. "I hate the fuckin' daffodils / I hate the blue remembered hills." He's loop the loop. Mind you, I'm glad he's given up archery. Oh God, look at the time. What am I doin' sittin' here talkin' and *he*'ll be in for his tea, won't he. An' what's he like? My feller. What's he like, wall? Well, he likes everything to be as it's always been. Like his tea always has to be on the table as he comes through that door. If the plate isn't landin' on the mat, there's ructions. I've given up arguin'. I said to him, once, I said, "Listen, Joe. If your tea isn't on the table at the same time every night it doesn't mean that the pound's collapsed y' know, or that there's been a world disaster. All it means, Joe, is that one of the billions of human bein's on this planet has to eat his tea at a different time." Well, did it do any good? I could've been talkin' to that. Couldn't I, wall?

Pause

I always said I'd leave him when the kids grew up. But by the time they'd grown up there was nowhere to go. Well, you don't start again at forty-two, do y'? They say, don't they, they say once you've reached your forties life gets a bit jaded an' y' start to believe that the only good things are things in the past. Well, I must have been an early developer, I felt like that at twenty-five. I'm not sayin' he's bad, my feller. He's just no bleedin' good. Mind you, I think most of them are the same, aren't they? I mean they're lovely at first. Know, when they're courtin' y'. Y' know, before you've had the horizontal party with them, oh they're marvellous then. They'll do anything for y'. Nothin' is too much trouble. But the minute, the very minute, after they've first had y' — their behaviour starts to change. It's like that advert, isn't it? I was watchin' it the other night — y' know, Milk Tray Man. Oh, he's marvellous, isn't he? Y' see him, he dives off a thousand foot cliff an' swims across two miles of water, just to drop off a box of chocolates. An' y' learn from that that the lady loves Milk Tray. And that the lady's been keepin' her legs firmly closed. Because if she hadn't, if he'd had his way with her he wouldn't go there by divin' off a thousand foot cliff an' swimmin' through a ragin' torrent. He'd go by bus. An' there'd be no chocolates. If she mentioned the chocolates that he used to bring he'd say "Oh no. I've stopped bringin' y' chocolates, babe, 'cos y' puttin' a bit too much weight on." D' y' know, when y' think about it, Cadbury's could go out of business if women didn't hold back a bit. I don't hate men. I'm not a feminist. Not like Jane. Jane's my mate. Now, she's a feminist. Well, she likes to think she is, y' know she reads *Cosmopolitan* an' says that all men are potential rapists. Even the Pope. Well, Jane does hate men. She divorced her husband, y' know. I never knew him, it was before I met Jane. Apparently she came back from work one mornin' an' found her husband in bed with the milkman. With the milkman, honest to God! Well, apparently, from that day forward Jane was a feminist. An' I've noticed, she never takes milk in her tea. I haven't known Jane all that long, be she's great. She's goin' to Greece for a fortnight. Next month she's goin'. God, what will I do for two weeks? She's the only one who keeps me sane. Jane's the only one I ever talk to, apart from the wall — isn't she, wall? She is. I said to her this mornin', "Jane, I won't half miss y' ". You know what she said to me? "I want you to come with me."

She laughs

Silly bitch. Hey, wall, wall, imagine the face on "him". Imagine the face if he had to look after himself for two weeks. Jesus, if I go to the bathroom for five minutes he thinks I've been hijacked.

She takes a sip of her wine

Oh, it's lovely, that. It's not too dry. Some of it'd strip the palate off y', wouldn't it? But this is lovely.

She takes another sip and savours it

It's nice. Wine. It's like it's been kissed by the sun. "He" doesn't drink wine. "He" says wine is nothin' but a posh way of gettin' pissed. I suppose it is really. But it's nice. Know what I'd like to do, I'd like to drink a glass of wine in a country where the grape is grown. Sittin' by the sea. Lookin' at the sun. But "he" won't go abroad. Well, y' see, he gets jet lag when we go to the Isle of Man. An' I wouldn't mind — we go by boat. We've been goin' there for fifteen years — he still won't drink the tap water. He's that type, Joe. Gets culture shock if we go to Chester. See, what Jane says is, he's entitled to his own mind an' that's fine. If he doesn't wanna go abroad, well that's up to him. But that shouldn't stop me goin'. If I want to. An' I know Jane's right. I know. It's logical. Dead logical. But like I said to her, "Jane, y' can't bring logic into this — we're talkin' about marriage." Marriage is like the Middle East, isn't it? There's no solution. You jiggle things around a bit, give up a bit here, take a bit there, deal with the flare-ups when they happen. But most of the time you just keep your head down, observe the curfew and hope that the cease-fire holds.

Pause

'Course, that was when Jane handed me the time bomb. She's only gone an' paid for me to go, hasn't she? She handed me the tickets this mornin'.

She goes to her bag and produces an air ticket from which she reads

"Bradshaw. S. Mrs. BD. Five-eight-one. Twenty-third of June. Nineteen hundred. From Man. to Cor." Jane said she didn't want to go on her own. She'd just got the money through from the sale of their house. Well, how the hell could I tell her it was impossible? I'll ... I'll give her the tickets back tomorrow. She'll easily find someone else to go with her. I shouldn't have taken the bloody tickets off her in the first place. Well, I tried to like, tried to expl ... to tell her it was impossible. But y' know what feminists are like. If something's impossible, that's the perfect reason for doin' it. Hey, wall, it'd be fantastic though, wouldn't it? I just lay his tea in front of him an' I turn away all dead cas, an' say " Oh, by the way, babe — I'm just poppin' off to Greece for a fortnight. Yeh. I just thought I'd mention it so's y' can put it in y' diary. You

won't mind doin' y' own washin' and cookin' for a couple of weeks, will y'?
There's nothing to it, doll. The white blob on the left of the kitchen is the
washin' machine an' the brown blob on the right is the cooker. An' don't get
them mixed up, will y', or y' might end up with socks on toast." Some chance,
eh wall? Some chance.

She returns the ticket to her bag

Y' know, if I said to him . . . if I said I was off to Greece for a fortnight, he'd
think it was for the sex. Wouldn't he, wall? Well . . . two women, on their own,
goin' to Greece. Well, it's obvious, isn't it? I wouldn't mind — I'm not even
particularly fond of it — sex — am I, wall? I'm not. I think sex is like
Sainsbury's — y' know, overrated. It's just a lot of pushin' an' shovin' an' y'
still come out with very little in the end. 'Course it would've been different if
I'd been born into the next generation, our Millandra's generation. 'Cos it's
different for them, isn't it? They discovered it, y' see, the clitoris. The Clitoris
Kids, I call them. And good luck to them, I don't begrudge them anythin'. But
when I was a girl we'd never heard of this clitoris. In those days everyone
thought it was just a case of "in out, in out, shake it all about", stars'd light up
the sky an' the earth would tremble. The only thing that trembled for me was
the headboard on the bed. But y' see, the clitoris hadn't been discovered then,
had it? I mean, obviously, it was always there, like penicillin, an' America. It
was there but it's not really there until it's been discovered, is it? Maybe I should
have married Christopher Columbus! I was about, about twenty-eight when I
first read all about it, the clitoris. It was dead interestin'. Apparently it was all
Freud's fault. Y' know, Sigmund. You see, what happened was, Freud had said
that there were two ways for a woman to have, erm, an orgasm. An', erm, the
main one could only be caused by havin' the muscles, inside, stimulated. An'
the other, erm, orgasm, it was supposed to be like an inferior, second-rate one,
was caused by the little clitoris. Now y' see, that's what Freud had said. An'
everyone had to believe him. Well, you would, wouldn't y'? I mean, Sigmund
Freud, who's gonna argue with Sigmund Freud. I mean, say you're just — just
standin' at the bus stop, you an' Sigmund Freud, the bus comes along, y' say
to him "Does this bus go to Fazakerley?" He nods an' says to y', "Yes, this is
one of the buses that goes to Fazakerley." Well, you'd get on the bus, wouldn't
you? But I'll tell y' what — you'd be bloody lucky if y' ever reached
Fazakerley. Because there's only *one* bus that goes to Fazakerley. The clitoris
bus. The other bus doesn't go anywhere near Fazakerley. But y' see, everyone
believed him an' they've been giving out wrong information for years, y' know

like they did with spinach. It's marvellous, isn't it— tellin' people there's two kinds of orgasm. It's like tellin' people there's two Mount Everests — some people stumble on to the real mountain while the rest of us are all runnin' up this little hillock an' wonderin' why the view's not very good when we get to the top. Well, when I first read about all this I was fascinated, wasn't I, wall? But y' know when you read a word for the first time an' you've never heard it spoken, you can get it wrong, can't y'? 'Know, pronounce it wrong. Like, when I was little there was a kid in our street called Gooey. Honest. Gooey. His mother used to go, "Gooey. Y' tea's ready, Gooey. Come on in, Gooey." Well, y' see, when she'd been lookin' for a name for him she'd been readin' this American magazine an' she saw this name, G.U.Y. Guy. But she thought it was pronounced Gooey. So that's what she christened him. Gooey McFadden, he was called. Well, it was the same with the clitoris. When I first read the word I thought it was pronounced clitoris. I still think it sounds nicer that way, actually. Clitoris. That even sounds like it could be a name, doesn't it? Clitoris. "Oh, hi-ya Clitoris, how are y'? Oh, really. Listen Clitoris, wait till I tell y' ... "

She thinks about it

Oh, shut up, wall. I think it sounds nice. Why not? There's plenty of men walkin' round called "Dick". Well, anyway, that's how I thought it was pronounced when I first mentioned it to Joe. We were sittin' in the front room an' I said, "Joey. Joe, have you ever heard about the clitoris?". He didn't even look up from his paper. "Yeh", he said, " but it doesn't go as well as the Ford Cortina."

Pause

Wait till he finds out he's gettin' chips an' egg for his tea tonight. Well, it's Thursday, isn't it? And on Thursday it has to be mince. It's the eleventh commandment, isn't it? Moses declared it. "Thou shalt give thy feller mince every Thursday and if thou doesn't, thy feller will have one big gob on him all night long." What will he be like, wall? What will he be like when he sees it's only chips an' egg? An' I wouldn't mind, it's not even my bloody fault about the mince. Well, I gave it the dog, y' see. This dog at the place I work. Well, it's a bloodhound, y' see. But this couple I work for— they're vegans. Y' know, the vegetarian lunatic fringe — the Marmite Tendency I call them. Well, they've brought up this bloodhound as a vegetarian. Well, it's not natural, is it? I mean, if God had wanted to create it as a vegetarian dog he wouldn't have

created it as a bloodhound, would he? He would have made it as a grapejuice
hound. But this dog is a bloodhound. It needs meat. Well, it was just on
impulse, really. I'm there, today, an' I looked at this dog an' all's I could think
about was the pound an' a half of best mince that's in me bag. Well, d' y' know,
I think it was worth what I'll have to put up with from "him" tonight; just to see
the look on that dog's face as it tasted meat for the first time. 'Course, I don't
think Joe'd quite see it that way. "Y' did what? What did y' do? Y' give it to
the dog? You've gone bloody mental, woman. Is this it? Have y' finally gone
round the pipe?"

She adopts a rather grand gesture and voice

"Yes, Joseph, I rather think I have. I have finally gone loop the facking loop.
I have become crazy with joy, because today Jane gave me the opportunity of
getting away for a fortnight. Joe! I am to travel to Greece with my companion.
Our departure is less than three weeks hence and we shall be vacationing for
some fourteen days. And now I must away, leaving you to savour your chips
and your Chuckie egg whilst I supervise the packing of my trunk."

She drops the pose

Our Brian was round before. I showed him the tickets. Didn't I, wall? An' what
did he say? "Mother, just go. Forget about me father, forget about everythin',
just get yourself on the plane an' go."

She laughs

Well, that's how he is, our Brian; you wanna do somethin', you just do it.
Bugger the consequences. He's a nutcase. But he couldn't care less. An' he's
always been the same. He was like that when he was a little kid, when he was
at school. Hey, wall, remember the nativity play? Oh God. Our Brian was only
about eight or nine an' the school had given up with him. The teachers just said
he was loop the loop an' that was that. I agreed with them. But the headmaster,
the headmaster was fascinated by our Brian. He like, like studied him. He said
to me, "There's no malice in the child, no malice whatsoever but it would appear
that Brian has no concept of consequences. I think what we have to do with
Brian is to try and give him more responsibility and so I've decided to give him
the star part in the nativity play this year." Well, when Brian learned he'd got
the part of Joseph he was made up with himself. Ah, God love him, he thought

he'd been picked 'cos he was great at actin' an' I couldn't say anythin' because it was workin', y' see, this psychology. All the time he's rehearsin' this nativity play his behaviour is fantastic; the headmaster's made up with him. I'm made up with him, the teachers up with him. An' he's made up with himself. He's practisin', every night in his room —

On one note

"We are weary travellers on our way to Bethlehem an' my wife is having a baby and we need rest at the inn for the night." Well, the day of the show, I got down to the school, the play started an' it was lovely, y' know, all the little angels come on an' they all have a sly little wave to their mams. Then it was our Brian's entrance; he comes on an' he's pullin' this donkey behind him — it's like this hobby-horse on wheels. An' perched on top of it is this little girl, takin' the part of the Virgin Mary an' she's dressed beautiful, y' know, her mother's really dolled her up to be the part. An' she's givin' a little wave to her mam. So Brian gives the donkey a bit of a tug because he's takin' it dead serious an' he doesn't believe they should be wavin' to their mams. He's up there, he's actin' like he might win the Oscar — y' know, he's mimin' givin' hay to the donkey an' he's pattin' it on the head. Well, the headmaster turned round an' smiled at me. I think he was as proud of our Brian as I was. Well, Brian gets to the door of the inn and he goes "Knock, knock, knock" an' the little Innkeeper appears. Our Brian starts "We are weary travellers on our way to Bethlehem an' my wife is havin' a baby an' we need to rest for the night at the inn." So the little feller playin' the Innkeeper pipes up: "You cannot stay at the inn because the inn is full up an' there is no room in the inn." An' then our Brian is supposed to say somethin' like: "Well, we must go an' find a lowly cattle shed an' stay in there." Then he's supposed to go off pullin' the donkey an' the Virgin Mary behind him. But he didn't. Well, I don't know if it's the Virgin Mary, gettin' up our Brian's nose, because she's spent the whole scene wavin' to her mother, or whether it was just that our Brian suddenly realized that the part of Joseph wasn't as big as it had been cracked up to be. But whatever it was, instead of goin' off pullin' the donkey, he suddenly turned to the little Innkeeper an' yelled at him: "Full up? Full up? But we booked!" Well, the poor little Innkeeper didn't know what day of the week it was. He's lookin' all round the hall for someone to rescue him an' his bottom lip's beginnin' to tremble an' our Brian's goin', "Full up? I've got the wife outside, waitin' with the donkey. She's expectin' a baby any minute now, there's snow everywhere in six-foot drifts an' you're tryin' to tell me that you're full up?" Well, the top brass on the front row are

beginnin' to look a bit uncomfortable — they're beginnin' to turn and look at
the headmaster an' our Brian's givin' a perfect imitation of his father, on a bad
day; he's beratin' anythin' that dares move. The little Innkeeper's lip is goin'
ten to the dozen an' the Virgin Mary's in floods of tears on the donkey. Well,
the Innkeeper finally grasps that the script is well out of the window an' that he
has to do somethin' about our Brian. So he steps forward an' he says, "Listen,
mate, listen! I was only jokin'. We have got room really. Y' can come in if y'
want." An' with that the three of them disappeared into the inn. End of nativity
play an' end of our Brian's actin' career. Me an' our Brian, we sometimes have
a laugh about it now, but at the time I could have died of shame. It was all over
the papers: "Mary And Joseph Fail To Arrive In Bethlehem." I was ashamed.

Pause

It's no wonder really, that I've never travelled anywhere meself; it must be God
punishin' me for raisin' a child who managed to prevent Mary an' Joseph
reachin' their destination. An' there was me when I was a girl — the only thing
I ever wanted to do was travel. I always wanted to be a — a courier. Or an air
hostess. But it was only the clever ones who got to do things like that. When I
got my final report from school the headmistress had written at the bottom of
it: "I can confidently predict that Miss Valentine" — that was me maiden name
— "I can confidently predict that Miss Valentine will not go far in life. I feel this
is just as well for, given her marks in geography, she would surely get lost." She
was a mare, that headmistress. She used to come into assembly sometimes an'
ask like a spot question, an' whoever got it right would get loads of house-
points, an' it was nearly always Marjorie Majors who got it right — she took
private elocution lessons an' she left school with just under four billion house-
points. One day, we were all standin' there in assembly an' this headmistress
appeared; "A question," she said to everyone, "a question: what was man's most
important invention?" Well, every hand in the hall shot up. "Me, miss", "I
know, miss", "Miss, miss, me, miss". An' my hand was up with the rest of them
because for once I knew the answer. But this headmistress, she took one look
at me an' said, "Oh, put your hand down, Shirley, you won't know the answer",
an' she started goin' round the hall, the grin on her face gettin' smugger an'
smugger as she got answers like, "the sputnik", "the cathode ray tube", "the
automatic washin' machine". Even the clever ones were gettin' it wrong —
even Marjorie Majors. But I kept my arm up there in the air because I knew I
had the right answer. I'd got it from me dad, an' he'd got it from the
Encyclopaedia Britannica. Ah, y' know me dad, he was still goin' on about that

Encyclopaedia Britannica when he was on his death-bed. "How can those kids of mine be so thick when I bought them the *Encylopaedia Britannica*?" He got a lot of pleasure out of it, though. He'd sit there for hours readin' it an' he'd try to impress us all with these dead odd facts. An' I'd remembered him sayin' about man's most important invention because it was so ordinary. So I'm stood there in assembly, me arm stuck up in the air, an' I'm like the cat with the cream because this headmistress has done the length an' breadth of the hall an' still no-one's come up with the right answer. Well, I'm the only one left so she turns to me an' she says, "All right then, Shirley, come on, you might as well get it wrong along with everyone else. Do you remember the question, Shirley — what was man's most important invention?" Well, I paused, y' know, savourin' the moment, knowin' I was on the brink of receivin' at least forty-three thousand house-points an' a blessin' from the Pope. But when I said, "the wheel", it was like this headmistress had been shot in the back. I thought maybe she hadn't heard me squeaky little voice so I said it again, louder: "The wheel, miss. Man's most important invention was ——" But I never got to finish because I was cut off by this scream from the headmistress. "*You*," she yelled, "you must have been told that answer!" I just stood there, reelin' with shock. An' I tried to ask her, to say — to say, how — how the bloody hell else was I supposed to know the right answer? But she wouldn't listen. She just ignored me an' told the demented music teacher to get on with playin' the hymn. An' all me house-points, an' me blessin' from the Pope, just disappeared before me eyes as she led the hall into singin' "Glad That I Live Am I". I was never really interested in school after that. I became a rebel. I wore me school skirt so high y' would've thought it was a serviette. I was marvellous. I used to have the chewy goin' all day, like that ...

she chews

... an' I'd just exude boredom out of every pore. I hated everythin'. "Oh, I hate him", "Oh, I hate her", "I hate this, I hate that". "It's garbage", "It's last", "It's crap". "I hate it." But I didn't hate anythin', y' know. The only thing I hated was me. I didn't want to be a rebel. I wanted to be nice. I wanted to be like Marjorie Majors. I used to pick on her somethin' rotten an' I really wanted to be like her. Can't y' be evil when you're a kid? I saw her a few weeks ago, Marjorie Majors. Didn't I, wall? I hadn't even heard of her for years. I'm in town, loaded down with shoppin', an' what's the first thing that always happens when y' in town loaded down with shoppin'? Right. The heavens opened. An' it's funny the way all these things are linked but they are; once you're in town, loaded with shoppin' bags, caught in a deluge — it always follows that every bus ever made disappears off the face of the earth. Well, I'm standin' there, like a drowned rat, me hair's in ruins an' I've got mascara lines runnin' from me face to me feet, so I thought I might as well trudge up to the *Adelphi* an' get a taxi. 'Course, when I got there the taxis had gone into hidin' along with the buses. Well, I'm just rootin' in me bag, lookin' for somethin' to slash me wrists with when this big white car pulls up to the hotel an', of course, I'm standin' right by a puddle an' as the wheels go through it, half the puddle ends up over me an' the other half in me shoppin' bags. Well, all I wanted to do by this time was scream. So I did. I just opened me mouth, standin' there in front of the hotel an' let out this scream. I could've been arrested but I didn't care. Well, I was in mid-scream when I noticed this woman get out the white car an' start comin' towards me. An' she's dead elegant. Y' know, she's walkin' through this torrential rain an' I guarantee not one drop of it was landin' on her. But the second she opened her mouth I knew who she was. I'd recognize those elocution lessons anywhere. "Forgive me for asking," she said, "but didn't you used to be Shirley Valentine?" I just stood there, starin'. And drippin'. "It is," she said, "it's Shirley." An' the next thing, she's apologizin' for half drownin' me an' she's pullin' me into the hotel an' across the lobby an' into this lounge that's the size of two football pitches. Well, she's ordered tea an' I'm sittin' there, rain water drippin' down me neck an' plastic carrier bags round me feet, an' I'm thinkin', "Well, Marjorie, you've waited a long time for your revenge but you've got me good style now, haven't y' ? Well, go on, spare me the torture, just put the knife in quick an' let's get it over with; come on, tell me all about you bein' an air hostess on Concorde." But she didn't say anythin'. She just sat there, lookin' at me, y' know, really lookin' at me. I thought I'm not gonna let her milk it so I said, "You're an air hostess these days, aren't y', Marjorie? Oh yes, I hear it's marvellous. You travel all over the world, don't you?" But she still just kept on lookin' at me. The waitress was just puttin' the tea an' cakes on the table in front of us. I said to her: "This is my friend Marjorie. We were at school together. Marjorie's an air hostess." "An air hostess?" Marjorie suddenly said, "Darling, whatever gave you that idea? I certainly travel widely but I'm not an air hostess. Shirley, I'm a hooker. A whore." Marjorie Majors — a high-class hooker! "Oh really, Marjorie," I said, "an' all that money your mother spent on elocution lessons." By this time the waitress was pourin' the tea into the cream buns! Well, me an' Marjorie — God, we had a great afternoon together. She didn't come lordin' it over me at all. Y' know, she told me about all the places she works — Bahrain, New York, Munich. An' d' y' know what she told me? When we were at school — she wanted to be like me. The two of us, sittin' there at the *Adelphi*,

one's like somethin' out of *Dynasty*, one's like somethin' out the bagwash an'
we're havin' a great time confessin' that all those years ago, we each wanted to
be the other. I was sad when I thought about it. Like the two of us could have
been great mates — y' know, real close. We didn't half get on well together, that
afternoon in the *Adelphi*. We were rememberin' all kinds. I could've sat there
for ever — neither of us wanted to leave. But then the time caught up with us
an' Marjorie had to get her plane. An' y' know somethin' — she didn't want to
go. Paris, she had to go to, Paris, France, an' she didn't want to go. An' — an'
on the way out — d' y' know what she did? She leaned forward an' just kissed
me — there on the cheek — an' there was real affection in that kiss. It was the
sweetest kiss I'd known in years. An' then she held my shoulders an' looked at
me an' said, "Goodbye, Shirley. Goodbye, Shirley Valentine".

Pause

On the way home, on the bus, I was cryin'. I don't know why. I'm starin' out
the window, tears trippin' down me cheeks. An' in me head there's this voice
that keeps sayin', "I used to be Shirley Valentine. I used to be Shirley Valentine
... I used to be Shirley ..."

And, indeed, she is now crying

What happened? Who turned me into this? I don't want this. Do you remember
her, wall? Remember Shirley Valentine? She got married to a boy called Joe an'
one day she came to live here. An' — an' even though her name was changed
to Bradshaw she was still Shirley Valentine. For a while. She still ... knew who
she was. She used to ... laugh. A lot. Didn't she? She used to laugh with Joe —
when the pair of them did things together, when they made this kitchen together
an' painted it together. Remember, wall? Remember when they first painted
you an' — an' the silly buggers painted each other as well. Stood here, the pair
of them, havin' a paint fight, coverin' each other from head to foot in yellow
paint. An' then the two of them, thinkin' they're dead darin', gettin' in the bath
— together. And the water was so yellow that he said it was like gettin' a bath
in vanilla ice-cream. And Shirley Valentine washed his hair ... and kissed his
wet head ... and knew what happiness meant. What happened, wall? What
happened to the pair of them — to Joe, to Shirley Valentine? Did somethin'
happen or was it just that nothin' happened? It would be ... easier to understand
if somethin' had happened, if I'd found him in bed with the milkman, if — if
there was someone to blame. But there's nothin'. They got married, they made

a home, they had kids and brought them up. And somewhere along the way the boy called Joe turned into "him" and Shirley Valentine turned into this and what I can't remember is the day or the week or the month or the ... when it happened. When it stopped bein' good. When Shirley Valentine disappeared, became just another name on the missin' persons' list.

She makes a partially successful attempt to change gear

He says he still loves me, y' know. But he doesn't. It's just somethin' he says. It's terrible — "I love you" — isn't it? Like — like it's supposed to make everythin' all right. You can be beaten an' battered an' half-insane an' if you complain he'll say, he'll say, "What's wrong, y' know I love you". "I love you." They should bottle it an' sell it. It cures everythin'. An' d' y' know somethin'? I've always wondered ... why ... it is that if somebody says, "I love you", it seems to automatically give them the right ... to treat you worse ... than people they only like, or people they don't like at all, or people they couldn't care less about. See — see, if I wasn't my feller's ... wife, if I was just a next-door neighbour or the man in the paper shop — he'd talk to me nice. An' he doesn't say he loves the next-door neighbour or the feller in the paper shop — he says he loves me! An' he doesn't talk nice to me. When he talks to me at all. It's funny, isn't it — "I love you".

Pause as she begins the final stage in the cooking of the meal

An' I know what you're sayin'. You're sayin' what Jane always says — why don't I leave? An' the fact of the matter is — I don't know why. I don't know why anyone should put up with a situation in which a forty-two-year old woman has the opportunity of fulfillin' a dream — of travellin', just a little bit, just two weeks of the year — an' can't do it. I don't know why ... I just know that if y' described me to me, I'd say you were tellin' me a joke. I don't know why I stay. I hate it. I hate the joke of it. I hate a life of talkin' to the wall. But I've been talkin' to the wall for more years than I care to remember now. An' I'm frightened. I'm frightened of life beyond the wall. When I was a girl I used to jump off our roof. For fun. Now I get vertigo standin' up in high-heeled shoes. I'm terrified, if y' want to know. I'm terrified that if I left him, I'd have nowhere to go, an' I'd find that there was no place for me in the life beyond the wall. They'd kept a place reserved for me. For a while. But when it seemed I wasn't comin' back they gave the place to someone else — maybe someone younger, someone who could still talk the language of the place beyond the wall. So I stay. Here. An' — an' if I have to give up goin' to Greece — well ... sod it. I mean, after all, what's the Acropolis? It's only an old-fashioned ruin, isn't it? It's like the DJs say, isn't it? "We're all scousers — there's nothing wrong with us — we've always got a laugh an' a joke, haven't we? They're not like us in London, are they? Not like us in Greece, are they? Greece? Y' know what Greece is, don't y', love? Greece is what y' cook his egg an' chips in."

She laughs. Pause

An' anyway, another bottle of Riesling, I'll be able to pretend this is Greece. Hey, wall ... look.

She goes to the window

Look at that sun an' the way it's shinin'. Look at the sea, the sea. Smell the honeysuckle. Can't y' just taste those olives, those grapes. Look, wall, look at that woman, that lovely woman — doesn't she look serene, sittin' beneath a parasol, at a table by the sea, drinkin' wine in a country where the grape is grown.

As she lays a plate on the table, the back door opens

Black-out

SCENE 2

The kitchen. Three weeks later

A suitcase stands in the kitchen. Shirley enters. She is dressed in a fairly formal and attractive two-piece suit, wears high heels and carries a hat which she places on top of the suitcase, and a large leather handbag/shoulder bag which she places on top of one of the work surfaces. Throughout the scene she constantly double and even triple checks details of the kitchen, contents of cupboards, whereabouts of utensils. When first she enters she is in a state of nervous agitation

SHIRLEY

Guess where I'm goin' ? Jane's booked a taxi to take us to the airport. She's pickin' me up at four o'clock.

Suddenly

Four o'clock.

She checks the clock and her watch

Oh jeez, oh jeez. Passport. Passport.

She checks the contents of her handbag

Passport, tickets, money. Passport, tickets, money. Yeh. Oh God, oh God, please say it will be all right. Oh, I feel sick. Those travel pills mustn't be workin' — I still feel sick an' I've taken four already. An' I've only travelled up an' down the stairs. Oh God, passport, tickets, money, passport. I got a full one, a proper passport. Well, you never know, Shirley — it could be the start of somethin' — this year Greece, next year . . . the world.

She slaps the passport shut with a cry of strained anguish

Oh. I know I should have told him. I know it would have been easier if I'd told him. It wouldn't though, would it, wall ? If I'd told him he would have talked me out of it. He would have found a way. He would have made me feel guilty. Guilty? As if I don't feel guilty enough as it is. Three weeks, secretly gettin' all me things ready. It's been like livin' in bleedin' Colditz with a tunnel beneath the floorboards an' every soddin' sound y' think it's the SS, comin' for y' — they've found out about the tunnel.

She looks up

God. God, I know . . . I'm bein' cruel. I know I'll have to pay for it, when I get back. But I don't mind payin' for it then. Just . . . just do me a big favour, God, an' don't make me have to pay for it durin' this fortnight. Don't let anythin' happen to our Millandra, our Brian. An' keep Joe safe. Please.

Pause

Three weeks secretly ironin' an' packin' an' cookin' all his meals for this two weeks. They're all in the freezer. Me mother's gonna come in an' defrost them an' do his cookin'. With a bit of luck "he" won't even notice I'm not here. Oh, I'll have to leave him a note. "Gone to Greece, back in two weeks." Oh, you should've told him. Y' should have, Shirley. Shirley, y' silly bitch. How could you have told him an' still been able to go? I know, I know. An' look what happened over his chips an' egg. I know, I know.

Pause

Keep thinkin' about the chips an' egg, keep thinkin' about the... It was that that decided me, wasn't it, wall? I'd cooked those chips lovely, hadn't I? In oil. An' they were free range those eggs. I mean, all right, so he was expectin' mince but... he sits down at that table, doesn't he, an' he looks at this plate of egg an' chips. Just looks. Doesn't make any effort to pick up his knife an' fork. He sits there, with this dead quizzical look on his face, an' he's starin' at the plate, studyin' it, y' know as though it contains the meanin' of life. Well, I just ignored him, didn't I? I just sat there, at the other end of the table. Well, eventually, he goes, "What's this? What. Is. This?" I said to him, I said, "Well, when I cooked it, it was egg an' chips, an' as neither of us is Paul Daniels I'm assuming it still is egg an' chips." Well, he leaned back in his chair an' he said " I am not ... eating shite", honest to God, an' he pushed the plate the entire length of the table. Well, I'm sitting there, then, aren't I? With a lap full of egg an' chips. I've got yolk drippin' down me leg an' "he" has started talkin' to the fridge. 'Cos he does that, when he's narked, doesn't he, wall? If he's in a real nark he always talks to the cooker or the fridge or the mantelpiece. "I'm pullin' me tripe out from mornin' till night", he's tellin' the fridge, "an' what does she give me when I get home". Well, of course, the fridge never answers him so whenever he asks it a question, he always answers it himself. He always goes — "I'll tell y' what she gives me. Chips an' egg, chips an' fuckin' egg she gives me." Well, I don't know what possessed me but while he was screamin' at the fridge, I picked meself up from the table, cleaned meself down as best I could, got hold of a pen an' wrote, across the wall, in big letters — GREECE. He didn't even notice,' cos by this time he's givin' the cooker an' the fridge his impression of Arthur Scargill deliverin' the Gettysburg Address. Well, I just walked out. I got me coat an' went round to our Millandra's flat. But there was no-one in. I just walked round the block a few times. I was gonna phone Jane, but all the phones were out of order. They always are, aren't they? Well, they are round here — even the vandals are complainin'. I must have walked round for about an hour. I wanted to go an' see someone, someone I could talk to. But there wasn't anyone. I never felt so alone in me whole life. I used to know so many people. Where does everyone go to ? In the end I just came back here. He'd been to a Chinese take-away. "What's that?" he said to me, pointin' at the wall. "It's a place," I said. "It's a place I'm goin' to." "I'm not goin' to no Greece," he said. "If that's why I'm not gettin' fed properly, because you're savin' up for a foreign holiday, y' can forget it." Well, that's when I started laughin'. I ended up — I was hysterical — I ended up rollin' on the kitchen floor. He just stepped over me, walked out. But I couldn't stop laughin' because I knew then. I knew I was gonna do it. I knew I was gonna go to Greece. An' everythin' went marvellous, didn't it ? I made all the arrangements, got me passport. I was quite impressed with meself. So yesterday I thought I'd nip into town an' get a few last- minute things, know the way y' do ? Well, as I passed Marks and Spencer's I looked in the window an' y' know they had some lovely underwear on display, y' dead silky. A little bit Janet Reger but only half the price. Well, normally I'm a bit conservative — next to the skin as it were — but I thought, oh, go on, give y'self a treat, it's the sort of stuff that'd be nice and cool in a hot climate. So I get into Marks, I bought a new bra, a couple of slips, a few pairs of pants an' I'm standin' there waitin' for them to be wrapped. Well, who comes up to me but "her" from next door. Gillian. Well, what's she like, wall ? What's Gillian like? I'm not sayin' she's a bragger, but if you've been to Paradise, she's got a season ticket. Y' know she's that type — if you've got a headache, she's got a brain tumour. "Oh, hello, Shirley," she says, 'cos that's how she talks, know she begrudges y' the breath. "Hello, Shirley, oh they're nice," she said, spottin' me little garments. "It's marvellous what they can do with man-made fibres these days, isn't it ?" An' she's pickin' up one of me slips y' know, havin' a really good gawp at it. "You'd almost think it was silk. If you weren't familiar with the real thing." I said to meself, "Keep your mouth shut, Shirley." Because y' can't win with her. Well, she dropped the slip back on the counter an' then she said, " But I suppose they will look quite nice on your Millandra". Well, I know I should've kept me mouth shut but that got me really riled an' I suddenly heard meself sayin', " Oh no, Gillian, these aren't for Millandra, I'm buyin' these for meself. Of course, I shan't be wearin' them for meself, I shall be wearin' them for my lover." Well, her jaw dropped into her handbag. For once she couldn't top it an' I got a bit carried away then. I heard meself sayin', "Yes, Gillian, we fly out tomorrow, my lover and I, for a fortnight in the Greek Islands — just two weeks of sun, sand, taramasalata an' whatever else takes our fancy. Well, I must be goin', Gillian — I've still got a few things to buy. I don't suppose you've noticed which counter the suspender belts are on ? Oh, well,

never mind, I'll find them. Ta-ra, Gillian", an' I was off before she could get
her wits together an' tell me about the two-year fling she's been havin' with
Robert Redford. 'Course, all the way home on the bus I'm thinkin' "Oh, you
silly bitch, why did you say that? What happens if she calls round tonight —
while "he"'s in? What happens if she just lets it slip?" 'Cos she's like that,
Gillian, y' know she's got more news than Channel Four. But when I got home
I forgot all about Gillian. When I got home, what was waitin' for me? Our
Millandra, with all her bags an' cases. "I hate that Sharron-Louise," she said.
"She's a mare. Mother, I've come back to live with you." Well, I'm stood here
lookin' at her, me jaw's dropped half-way to Australia. "Mother," she says,
"Will y' make me some Horlicks an' toast —like y' used to?" Then she was off.
Up the stairs to her old room. Well, I made the toast an' the Horlicks — took
it up to her. She's got herself into bed, sittin' there propped up with two pillows,
readin' her old *Beano* annuals. "I love you, Mother," she said, "I don't know
why I went to live with that cow in the first place — Mother, y' haven't put
enough sugar in the Horlicks, will y' get us another spoon?" Well, I go down,
get the sugar, bring it back, stir it up for her an' she's sayin' "We'll go down
town on Saturday, shall we, Mother? We'll do a bit of shoppin', eh Mother, just
you an' me". An' the thing is, I was noddin'. She hadn't been back ten minutes
an' I'd gone straight into bein' "Auto-Mother". She'd got me struttin' round
like R2 bleedin' D2. Well, it was when she asked me to bring the telly upstairs
for her that me head cleared. Instead of goin' downstairs again I sat on the edge
of the bed an' I said, "Millandra, I'm really pleased you've come back home
because I've missed y'. I mean, I've never said that or whinged an' whined
because, because I believe that kids have to have their own lives. But there's
many a time y' know, many a time that I would have loved to sit down with y'
an' talk, go to town with y', have a meal with y', share a laugh, just, like not as
your mother but as another human bein'. But I couldn't because you had your
own life, your own friends, your own interests — none of it to do with me."
"Well, we'll be able to do all that now," she said, "because I've come back
home." "And that's fantastic," I said. "An' you couldn't have picked a better
time — it'll be a great help havin' you here to look after your father." Well, this
look came on her face. "What's wrong with him?" she said. "Oh, there's nothin
wrong with him," I assured her, "but y' know with me not bein' here, with me
an' Jane goin' to Greece tomorrow." Well, d' y' know, it was like her hot water
bottle had sprung a leak. "What?" she yelled. "Yeh", I said, "I'm going to
Greece for a fortnight." "You," she said, "you goin' to Greece, what for?" "For
two weeks," I said. Well she flounces out of the bed. "That Jane one, an' you,"
she's goin', "in Greece. An' what's me father had to say about that?" Well,

when I said I hadn't told him, she went mental. She started gettin' dressed, "I think it's a disgrace," she's goin', "two middle-aged women goin' on their own to Greece — I think it's disgustin'." An' she's straight down the stairs an' on the phone, tellin' Sharron-Louise that she's comin' back to the flat. Well, I'm sittin' there upstairs an' then it suddenly struck me — her sayin' I was disgustin'. I mean she's jumpin' to the same conclusions as her father would. She thinks I'm just goin' off on a grab-a-granny fortnight. Well, I started to get narked. The more I thought about it, the more riled I got. I was gonna go down an' give her a piece of me mind but I heard the front door slam. I went to the window an' she's loadin' her things into a taxi. Well, I flung the window open an' I shouted, "Yes, that's right, Millandra — I'm goin' to Greece for the sex; sex for breakfast, sex for dinner, sex for tea an' sex for supper." Well, she just ignored me but this little cab driver leans out an' pipes up, " That sounds like a marvellous diet, love." "It is," I shouted back, " have y' never heard of it? It's called the 'F' Plan." Well, our Millandra slammed the taxi door an' off they went down the street. I just sat there in our Millandra's bedroom. I was livid at first but when I calmed down I just felt . . . felt like a real fool. All I could think about was Millandra sayin', "What for? You goin' to Greece — what for?" Kids — they can't half destroy your confidence, can't they? I'd spent three weeks tellin' meself I could do it, that I'd be all right, be able to go, be able to enjoy meself. I'd even convinced meself that I wasn't really that old, that me hips weren't really as big as I thought they were, that me belly was quite flat for a woman who's had two kids. That me stretch marks wouldn't really be noticeable to anyone but me. I'd even let that salesgirl at C&A sell me a bikini. But sittin' there on our Millandra's bed, after she'd said that — I suddenly had thighs that were thicker than the pillars in the Parthenon. Me stretch marks were as big as tyre marks on the M6 an' instead of goin' to Greece I should be applyin' for membership of the pensioners' club. I'm sittin' there thinkin', maybe our Millandra's right. "You goin' to Greece. What for?" Maybe she's right, maybe it is pathetic. What am I goin' for? I mean, it might be easier not to go, to stay here. Where I'm safe. Where's there's no risk. For three weeks I'd been buildin' up this marvellous picture of what it would be like, how I was goin' to feel with the sun on me an' the ocean everywhere. But after she'd said that I couldn't . . . couldn't get the picture back, into me mind. I couldn't bring back the feelin' I'd had. I just sat there thinkin', "Shirley you are one silly bitch. Just another stupid woman who thinks she can have an adventure, when the time for adventures is over." "What for?", I kept askin' meself. I thought about the bikini I'd bought an' I felt ashamed. I felt embarrassed at me own stupidity, at lettin' meself think it was possible. "What for?" "What am I goin' for?" An' of course the truth of the matter was that I was goin' for the excitement of not knowing; not knowing where I was goin', not knowing what would happen, not knowing what the place would be like or look like, not knowin' the foreign language I'd hear, not knowin', for the first time since before I could remember, exactly what the days would hold for me. It was the excitement of somethin' that was foreign, to me. The excitement of jumpin' off our roof. An' when our Millandra had said that, it was like, like she'd caught me, on the roof, just as I was about to jump an' she'd said, "Ey, you'll break your bloody neck. Get down off there an' don't be so stupid". An' I hesitated, an' in that moment I saw how big the drop was, an' how hard the ground was an' how fragile me bones were. An' I realized that I was too old for jumpin' off the roof. I went downstairs, to phone Jane, to phone me mother an' tell her she needn't bother comin' in for the fortnight. I'd even picked up the phone. But the doorbell went an' I put the phone down an' went to the door. Gillian was stood there. "Oh, hello Shirley," she said, "is Joe at home?" Well, I just laughed. "No, Joe's not in, Gillian. But listen, if you've come to spill the beans y' might as well . . ." But she just pushed past me, came into the house. "I don't want to spill any beans, Shirley," she said, " I just wanted to check that Joe wasn't in before I gave you this." An' she handed me this beautifully wrapped package. " I want you to have this, Shirley. It's never been worn. You see," she said, " I was never . . . brave enough. Oh, Shirley," she said, " how I wish I had. How I wish I'd had your . . . bravery." With that she went to the door. Just as she was goin' out she said to me — "You're brave, Shirley. I just want you to know, I think you're marvellous." An' she was gone. I opened up the package.

She opens her suitcase

It was this.

She produces a superb silk robe

Silk. Gillian was right — there's nothin' like the real thing. It must have been bought years an' years ago. It's got the original label — The Bon Marché. I didn't even dare try it on at first. I felt awful, about what I'd said to Gillian, about taking a lover. I mean, I didn't think she'd really believe me. But she had. Completely believed me. Gillian believed that it was perfectly possible for me to be some marvellous, brave, living woman. I got me mirror out an' looked at meself, an' tried to see the woman that Gillian had seen in me. In Gillian's eyes I was no longer Shirley the neighbour, Shirley the middle-aged mother, Shirley

Bradshaw. I had become Shirley the Sensational, Shirley the Brave, Shirley Valentine. An' even if I couldn't see it in the mirror, even if none of it was true about me takin' a lover an' all that rubbish — the point is that Gillian had believed it. Believed it was possible of me. I tried the robe on. It was perfect. It was beautiful. An' in that moment . . . so was I. In that moment our roof wouldn't have been high enough for me. I could have jumped off a skyscraper. An' now the day's here. An' I'm goin'. I'm goin' to the land beyond the wall. I'm gonna sit an' eat olives on a Greek seafront. An' I don't even like olives. But I might like them in Greece. They eat squid y' know. An' octopus — they do. An' I'm gonna eat it too. I don't care. I'm gonna do everythin'. I'm gonna try anything. Like I used to. Unafraid. Without fear of anythin' new. I'll be Shirley the Brave. 'Course, I'm terrified really. But I'm not gonna let it stop me from enjoyin' things. I don't mean I'm gonna be a girl again — because you can never be that; but instead of sayin' "Christ, I'm forty-two". I'm gonna say — "Shirley, you're only forty-two, isn't that marvellous".

She looks at herself in the mirror

Not bad, not bad. Oh, hold on, hold on.

She places the hat on her head and examines the effect in the mirror

What do you think, wall? Oh, shut up, wall, I'm not talkin' to you anymore.

She smiles at herself in the mirror

Well, that's it, Shirley — all dolled up an' ready to go. Case packed? Case packed. Passport, tickets, money? Passport, tickets, money.

She closes her handbag and sits with it, on the suitcase. She takes a last glance at the kitchen to see if everything has been left in order. It has

Four o'clock Jane's pickin' me up.

She looks at her watch

Twenty past two.

Black-out

ACT II

A Greek island

A secluded section of shore, dotted with rocks and baked by the Mediterranean sun. It is an underdeveloped corner of the bay, a place not yet appropriated by tourists. In the background we see a hint of the village and the taverna. The deep blue of the sky dominates. A white table with some chairs has been placed in this spot

When the CURTAIN *rises, the parasol is still folded. There is a piece of rush-matting laid out for sunbathing*

Shirley enters. She has bare feet and wears Gillian's robe over cut-down denims and a bikini top

SHIRLEY
I'll bet y' didn't recognize me, did y'? I hardly recognize meself these days. D' y' like me tan?

She opens the robe to display a deep tan

It's marvellous, isn't it? I love it here — don't I, rock?

She points to the rock

That's rock. We met the first day I got here, didn't we? Well, I didn't want to go down on to the beach, y' see. I thought I'd get a bit of a tan before I ventured on to the beach because — let's face it — I was so white. If I'd walked on to that beach when I first got here, they would have thought I'd just had a fresh coat of white emulsion. When I first arrived there was more glare comin' off me than there was off the sun. So what I did was I found this little place — I found you, didn't I, rock? I talked to you. Rock. He's got his name written all the way through him. 'Course, I talk to rock — but he doesn't talk back to me. Well he can't, can he? It's a Greek rock. It doesn't understand a bleedin' word I'm sayin'. I might have risked the beach if I'd been with Jane. But on me own I felt a bit — y' know, conspicuous. Jane met a feller, didn't she? Not here, on the plane — honest to God. An' the state of him. I wouldn't give y' tuppence a ton. Sporty type — y' know, all groin an' Adidas labels. Ooogh. Designer teeth he had. An' bloodshot eyes. Y' know when he smiled with these blazin' white teeth an' the bloodshot eyes, I said to Jane, "Oh, he must be a Liverpool supporter". She didn't like that. But I didn't care. I'd got past carin' to tell y' the truth. I mean, we were gonna do everythin' together. We hadn't even landed an' she's got herself fixed up. She only went to the loo. When she got back she said to me, "Erm, I've just been invited out to dinner. Tonight." Well, I looked at her. "Pardon," I said. "Yeh," she said, "I've just met this chap, sittin' up at the back. He's stayin' at a villa on the other side of the island an' he's invited me over for dinner. Tonight. Oh Shirley, you don't mind, do you?" Well, I didn't say anythin'. There was nothin' I could say, was there? I just stared out the window of the plane an' I thought, "D' y' know, if I had a parachute, I'd get off now." I even considered gettin' off without a parachute actually. 'Course, she was sayin' to me — "It's only for tonight. We'll still do all the things we planned, Shirley." But I knew. Me instinct told me I'd hardly see her again after that. An' I didn't want her to be spendin' time with me when she'd rather be elsewhere. I didn't want her pityin' me. "Listen, Jane," I said, "I think you've probably blown the feminist of the year award — so will y' just leave it out, right? Obviously," I said, "it's been a difficult time for you since your feller ran off with the milkman and now that you've got this opportunity I don't want y' to give even a thought to me. You just go off to his villa an' enjoy yourself an' give his olives a good pressing." D' y' know what she said to me? "Thanks for bein' so understandin'." An' she never came back that night, y' know. Or the next mornin'. She never came back for the first four days. They must've been marvellous olives. I was just left on me own. I was alone. But I wasn't lonely. Well, I'm an expert at it really. But what I found was — if you're a woman, alone, it doesn't half seem to upset people; like whenever I walked into the dinin'-room at the hotel it was like everyone was lookin' at me. I've got this little table to meself, an' it's lovely. I just love sittin' there, in the evenin'. But on the third day, I'm sat there, at me table. I've been sunbathin' all day, I'm glowin' like a lobster an' feelin' dead content an' quiet. I was in such a trance, I hadn't even noticed this woman come across. She was talkin' to me before I realized she was there. "We couldn't help notice you were alone, dear," she says to me. "Would y' like to come an' join us at our table? There is a spare place." Well, I was shattered. I didn't want to join anyone. I didn't wanna talk. I wanted to be quiet. But she's standin' there, waitin' for me to say somethin'. An' then I notice that the whole of the restaurant's waitin' to see what would happen to the woman on her own. Well, of course, I couldn't say no, could I? I mean, the woman was only bein' kind, wasn't she? But inside I was cursin'. Well, d' y' know, as I sat down at their table, with her an' her husband, it was like the whole restaurant let out this great sigh of relief, as if me bein' on me own had been like a great problem for everyone, an' now it had been solved, everyone could relax, everyone could talk louder an' laugh; I thought the waiters were gonna break into applause 'cos I'd been rescued from me loneliness by Jeanette an' Dougie. Jeanette an' Dougie Walsh — from Manchester. Well, I know the exact dimensions of her kitchen, the price of the new extension, the colour of the microwave an' the contents of the Hoover, an' we hadn't even started on the first course; it's a good job it wasn't soup — I would've put me head in it an' drowned meself. It wasn't until we got to the main course that they even acknowledged we were in Greece. An' then I wish they hadn't bothered. Everythin' was wrong — the sun was too hot for them, the sea was too wet for them, Greece too Greek for them. They were that type, y' know, if they'd been at the Last Supper they would have asked for chips. An' I wouldn't mind but the family on the next table joined in as well an' started complainin' about everythin'. An' I'm sittin' there dead embarrassed out of me mind because there's this poor Greek waiter tryin' to serve our main course an' he's got to listen to this lot goin' on about his country as though it's in the Fourth World. This feller on the table next to us is sayin' to Dougie, "'Ave y' not seent bloody fishin' boats they've out theer int bay? 'Ave y' not seen 'em, 'ave y' not? Bloody hell, what they like, love?" he says to his wife, "What did I say to you when I saw them boats int bay. I said to her, I did, I said them boats, if y' look at side of 'em ant find name of t' boatbuilder, I'll bet y' a pound to a penny it says Noah. Din't I? I bloody did. Ay." An' they're all roarin' with laughter. Well, I was so ashamed I couldn't keep me mouth shut any longer. "Excuse me," I said to the feller on the next table, "excuse me. You do watch the Olympic Games I take it? An' y' do know, I suppose, that it was the Greeks who invented the Olympic Games?" Well, they were all lookin' at me. "Oh yes," I said, "it was the Greeks who were responsible for the most important invention of all — the wheel." 'Course I didn't know if it had been invented by the Greeks, the Irish or the cavemen but I didn't care. Once I'd opened me mouth there was no stoppin' me. "The English," I'm goin', "the English? Don't talk to me about the English, because whilst the Greeks were buildin' roads an' cities an' temples, what were the English doin'? I'll tell y' what the English were doin', they were runnin' round in loin cloths an' ploughin' up the earth with the arse-bone of a giraffe." Well, I hadn't meant to get so carried away like. I suddenly realized how loud I'd been shoutin'. Everyone's lookin' at me — the feller an' his family on the next table have turned away an' Dougie an' Jeanette are sittin' there wonderin' why they asked this lunatic to join them. Well, Dougie obviously decides to use diversionary tactics an' he says to the waiter who's just walkin' away, "Hey, mate. What is this?" An' he points to his plate. The waiter says to him, "Eet ees calamares, sir." "Yeh, but what I'm askin' y'," Dougie says, "what I'm askin' y', is what is it?" "Erm ...eet's calamares, sir, eet's a type of er ... feesh." Well, Dougie looks at his plate an' he's not convinced. "It don't look much like fish to me," he says. "My wife's got a very delicate stomach. She's very particular about what she eats. Are you sure this is fish?" "Sir, I can ... promees you," says the waiter, "eet ees feesh. Eet ees feesh ... was pulled from the sea thees morning, by my own father. In a boat called *Noah*." Well, the silence at our table is deafenin'. We're all sittin' there eatin' an' no-one's sayin' a word. I'm feelin' like a right heel because I've upset them all an' I'm tryin' to think of somethin' to say that'll make it all right. Well y' know what it's like when — when there's one of those silences an' you've got to force yourself to find somethin' to say — you always come out with the wrong thing, don't y'? Well, what I said was, "The squid's very nice, isn't it?" The pair of them stopped eatin' an' looked at me. "Pardon me?" Jeanette said. "The squid," I said, pointin' to her plate, "the squid, the octopus, it's quite nice really, isn't ... ?" Well, it was funny the way Jeanette fainted. Y' know, sort of in slow motion. As she comes round I'm tryin' to apologize an' everythin', but they were off — out — away. They didn't eat in the hotel after that. Apparently they found this restaurant at the back of the hotel that does proper Greek food — doner kebabs. After dinner, whilst everyone else was makin' their way to the bar, I went up to me room an' grabbed me light coat an' I walked out of the hotel an' into this lovely night outside.

Pause, as she remembers it

Well that's when I met him. Y' know — Christopher Columbus. That's not his real name. His real name's Costas. But I call him Christopher. Christopher Columbus. I'll bet y' don't know why I call him that? It's because he's got a boat. Well, it's his brother's boat actually. And because it's er — he, we — discovered it. The island of clitoris. I'm terrible, aren't I? I suppose y' think I'm scandalous — a married woman, forty-two, got grown-up kids. I suppose y' think I'm wicked. Jane does. "Shirley," she said, "you're acting like a stupid teenager. I suppose the next thing you're going to tell me is that the earth trembled." "Trembled?" I said. "Jane, I thought there'd been an earthquake. It was at least point nine on the Richter Scale." "Oh spare me the details," she's goin', "spare me the details." Well she wasn't half jealous. But y' see, it wasn't my fault; if she hadn't gone off, with the walkin' groin, in the first place — I never would have met Christopher Columbus.

Pause

He kissed me stretch marks, y' know. He did. He said — he said they were lovely ... because they were a part of me ... an' I was lovely. He said — he said, stretch marks weren't to be hidden away; they were to be displayed, to be proud of. He said my stretch marks showed that I was alive, that I'd survived ... that they were marks of life.

Pause

Aren't men full of shit? I mean, can you imagine him, the mornin' after he's given me this speech — he wakes up an' he finds his belly has got all these lines runnin' across it? I mean, can y' see him? Rushin' to the mirror an' goin', "Fantastic. Fuckin' fantastic. I've got stretch marks. At last!" But the thing about him, the thing about Costas was, when he gave y' a load of guff — *he* believed it. What was marvellous about him was he never made y' feel at all threatened. An' he understood how to talk with a woman. That's the first thing I noticed about him. 'Cos, y' know, most men, really, they're no good at talkin' with women. They don't know how to listen or they feel that they have to take over the conversation. Like ... with most fellers, if you said somethin' like — like, "My favourite season is autumn." Well, most fellers'd go, "Is it? My favourite season's spring. See, what I like about spring is that in spring ..." Then y' get ten minutes of why he likes spring. An' you weren't talkin' about spring — you were talkin' about autumn. So what d' y' do. You end up talkin' about what he wants to talk about. Or you don't talk at all. Or you wind up talkin' to y'self. An' whichever way it works out it always ends up that there's no talkin' goin' on. It just becomes words. Words without meanin'. Words that get spoken ... but die ... because they have nowhere to go. But it wasn't like that with Costas. When I came out the hotel that night I just walked down the little esplanade. There was hardly a soul about, but I noticed the light was on in the taverna an' outside the front of it there's these tables, with white parasols. Well I'm sittin' there an' he came out to serve me. "Erm, excuse me," I said to him, "I know this sounds a bit soft but would you mind ... I mean would you object if I moved this table an' chair over there, by the edge of the sea?" Well, he looked at me for a minute. "You want," he said, "you want move table and chair to the sea? What for? You don't like here at my bar?" "Oh yeh," I said, "yeh, it's a lovely bar but — but I've just got this soft little dream about sittin' at a table by the sea." "Ah," he said, an' he smiled. "A dream, a dream. We move this table to the edge of the sea, it make your dream come true?" "Erm, yeh," I said. "I think so." "Then, is no problem. I move the table for you. And tonight when I serve in my bar, I say to customer — 'tonight, tonight I make someone's dream come true'." Well, I thought for a second he was bein' sarcastic — 'cos in England it would have been. But no, he carries the table an' chair over here an' he brings me out this glass of wine I've ordered. Well, I paid him an' thanked him but he said to me, "No, I thank you. Enjoy your dream", then he gave a little bow an' he was gone, back to the taverna, leavin' me alone with the sea an' the sky an' me soft little dream. Well, it's funny, isn't it, but y' know if you've pictured somethin', y' know, if you've imagined how somethin's gonna be, made a picture of it in your mind, well it never works out, does it? I mean for weeks I'd had this picture of meself, sittin' here, sittin' here, drinkin' wine by the sea; I even knew exactly how I was gonna feel. But when it got to it, it wasn't a bit like that. Because when it got to it, I didn't feel at all lovely an' serene. I felt pretty daft actually. A bit stupid an' — an' awfully, awfully old. What I kept thinkin' about was how I'd lived such a little life. An' one way or another even that would be over pretty soon. I thought to meself, my life has been a crime really — a crime against God, because ... I didn't live it fully. I'd allowed myself to live this little life when inside me there was so much. So much more that I could have lived a bigger life with — but it had all gone unused, an' now it never would be. Why — why do y' get ... all this life, when it can't be used? Why — why do y' get ... all these ... feelin's an' dreams an' hopes if they can't ever be used. That's where Shirley Valentine disappeared to. She got lost in all this unused life. An' that's what I was thinkin', sittin' there on me own, starin' out at the sea, me eyes open wide an' big tears splashin' down from them. I must've sat there for ages because the noise from the hotel bar had died away an' even the feller from the taverna was lockin' up for the night. He came to collect me glass. It was still full. I hadn't even taken a sip. He saw that I was cryin' but he didn't say anythin'. He just sat down , on the sand an' stared out at the sea. An' when I'd got over it, when it was all right to talk, he said, "Dreams are never in the places we expect them to be." I just smiled at him. "Come," he said, "I escort you back to your hotel." An' he did. An' he told me his name was Costas an' I told him my name was

Shirley. An' when we got to the front door of the hotel he said to me,
"Tomorrow, you want, to come with me? I take my brother's boat. We go all
round the island?" I just shook me head, "No," I said, "it's all right. You've been
dead kind as it is. Thank you." "Is no problem, I come for you, early." "No," I'm
goin', "thanks but ..." "You afraid?" he suddenly said. "No," I said, "but ... "
"You afraid," he said, nodding, "you afraid I make try to foak with you." I didn't
know where to put meself, but he just laughed. "Of course I like to foak with
you. You are lovely woman. Any man be crazy not to want to foak with you.
But I don't ask to foak. I ask you want to come my brother's boat — is different
thing. Foak is foak, boat is boat. I come fetch you tomorrow. I bring wine, I bring
food and we go. Tomorrow, I just make you happy. No need to be sad, no need
to be afraid. I give my word of honour I don't try to make foak with you." Well,
what could I say? "Well, I'll — erm — I'll see y' in the mornin' then." 'Course,
the next mornin' I've just got dressed. I'm sittin' in me room, there's this
knockin' on me door, I thought, "Oh Christ, he's come up to me room." Well,
I opened the door, an' guess what? Jane's back! "Shirley, I know I've been
awful but please, please forgive me. I'll make it up to you. Come on, it's still
early, let's go and hire a car and drive out round the island." Well, what could
I do? I mean she had paid for me to be there. If it hadn't been for Jane I never
would have been in Greece in the first place. She keeps askin' me if I forgive
her. "Of course I forgive y'," I said, an' she threw her arms round me then.
"Come on," she said, "let's put it all behind us now. Let's make today the real
start of our holiday. I know you've had an awful time and Shirley I'm sorry.
Have you just been sitting here in your room the past few days? I know you.
Without me being here I suppose you've just been sitting here talking to the
wall, haven't you?" "Well," I thought to meself, "how does she see me? Does
she think I'm an old-aged pensioner or a five-year-old child?" "I'll only be a few
minutes," she's sayin', "I'll just pick up a few things from my room." Well, it
was just as she got to the door that there was a knock on it. She pulled it open
an' Costas was there. She took one look at him an' said, "What is it, room
service? Did you order anything, Shirley?" But Costas just walked straight past
her an' into the room. "Shirley, Shirley, you come, you come. You late. I wait
for you on the quay. I already put the wine, the food on the boat. I stand, I wait
an' then I think, 'Ah, Shirley and me, we get to bed so late last night, Shirley
she must have oversleep.'" Well, the look on Jane's face could've turned the
milk. "Quickly now you get ready. Don't need bring much clothing. I wait on
quay for you. Hurry." An' as he passes Jane he goes, "Apology for interrupt-
ing you. Now you continue cleaning the room." Well, if Jane had kept her mouth
shut, if she hadn't tried to treat me like a child, I might have run after Costas an'

said I couldn't go, or could me friend come as well. But she said, "Shirley. What do you think you're playing at?" I didn't say a word. I just looked at her. She was goin' on about how I'd never been abroad before. When she got to the bit about, "men like that, these Greek islanders who are just waiting for bored, middle-aged women to fall into their ... " I just stormed straight past her an' out. I steered the boat, y' know. See me on that bridge — natural. I mean, I knew I wasn't the first woman on that boat an' I certainly wouldn't be the last. But I knew I was with a good man. I knew that whatever happened he wouldn't take anythin' from me. We sailed for miles an' miles. An' we talked. Properly. An' we didn't half laugh. We liked each other. An' isn't it funny, but if you're with someone who likes y', who sort of, approves of y', well y' like — like start to grow again. Y' move in the right way, say the right thing at the right time. An' you're not eighteen or forty-two or sixty-four. You're just alive. An' I know if I could have seen myself that day I would have said, "Look at that lovely woman, riding on the sea. Look at that lovely woman, swimming." Well, I know I'd left me swimmin' costume in the hotel. So what? We'd parked the boat an' was lookin' over the side. I said, "How deep do you think it is here, Costas?" "Mm. Maybe a thousand metres — maybe ten thousand metres, who knows. Maybe so deep it goes on forever." An' when I stood there, on the edge of the boat, naked as the day I was born, about to jump into this water that was as deep as forever, I felt as strong an' as excited an' as bloody mad as I did when I jumped off our roof. The two of us just splashed an' laughed an' swam in the water an' I knew Costas would keep his promise but I didn't want him to because it was the most natural thing in the world. So I swam up to him. An' I put me arms around him an' kissed him. An' that's when I nicknamed him Christopher Columbus. Mind you, I could just as easily have named him Andre Previn — I don't know where this orchestra came from. Later on, just lyin' there on the boat, with the sun beginnin' to dip towards the evenin', that's when the thought came to me. I tried to like, push it out of me head at first. Because it was too shocking. I kept tryin' to think of other things, to make this thought go away. But it wouldn't. It was just there in me head. An' this thought was: "If ... somehow ... if ... for ... some ... reason ... I ... didn't ... go ... back ... home ... who would really care? Would it cause anyone real suffering? Would it damage anyone? Who would miss — me? Why should I go back? Why should I go back an' become that woman again when — when that woman isn't needed anymore. Her job's done. She's brought up her kids." I mean, they'd say it was awful, it was terrible to have a mother who went on holiday an' never came back. I hadn't gone round the pipe. I hadn't. I hadn't fallen in love with Costas. It had been sweet. It had been lovely. It had been a day full of kindness. But I hadn't fallen in love with him. I'd fallen in love with the idea of livin'. An' every day, when I woke up, when I came down here with Jane, when we went an' had a coffee or a drink at Costas's taverna, when I was lyin' in me bed, just droppin' off to sleep, it was always there in me head — this shocking thought — "I'm not goin' back. I'm not goin' back."

Pause

An', of course, all the time I knew really. I knew I'd have to go back in the end. I knew that I was just one of millions before me who'd gone on a holiday an' had such a good time that they didn't want to go home. Because we don't do what we want to do. We do what we have to do. An' pretend it's what we want to do. An' what I wanted to do was to stay here and be Shirley Valentine. An' what I had to do was to go back there, back to bein' St Joan of the Fitted Units. An' all through the days, an' when I said goodbye to Costas, an' on the way to the airport, an' in the long queue for the check-in desk, I didn't know if I'd do what I wanted to do, or what I had to do. We were standin' there, in this queue, me an' Jane an' all the others who had to go back. An' I remembered this question I was gonna ask Jane. So I said to her, "Jane, Jane, why is it that there's all this unused life?" She just said it was because of men, it was all the fault of men, an' went back to readin' her magazine. An' I thought about it, an' I thought: "That's rubbish … it's not just men who do it to women. Because I've looked at Joe, an' I know it's the same for him. He had more life in him than he could use. An' so he carries all this … waste around with him. It's the same for everyone. I know it. When I'm out, when I'm in the shops, when I see people I grew up with, standin' there in the shop buyin' vegetables. An' we say how are y', we all say fine, an' we pretend we are because the vegetables are fresh an' we haven't had a cold this year an' our kids grew up with their limbs intact an' never got into trouble with the police. We say we're fine. An' we carry on an' on an' on until we die. An' most of us die … long before we're dead. An' what kills us is the terrible weight of all this unused life that we carry round." We'd got to the check-in desk. Me suitcase was on the conveyor belt with a tag on it, for England, for home. I stood there, just watchin' it as it moved away, along the conveyor belt an' through those flaps an' disappeared into this dark hole. An' I knew then. I knew I couldn't go with it … Jane just called out at first, as she saw me walkin' away. Then she realized, she knew an' she screamed at me to come back, to come back. All the people in the queue were lookin' at me. An' I knew they all wanted me to "come back, come back". But I just kept walkin', across the concourse. All I had left was me handbag, the clothes I stood up in, Gillian's robe, me passport an' a few drachmas. An' after I'd paid me bus fare, even the drachmas had gone.

Pause

When I walked up to the taverna, Costas was talkin' to this woman, sittin' on a bar stool. As I walked in I heard him sayin' to her: "You afraid? You afraid I want make try to make ——" The poor feller, he nearly dropped his olives when he saw me. "Don't worry, Costas," I said, "I haven't come back for you. I've come back for the job. The job in your taverna." Nearly three weeks I've been workin' there now. I get on well with the customers. Even the Dougies and Jeanettes, we get a pair of them every week, y' know. They come in, order a drink an' look all dead nervous at the menu. I always say to them, "Would you like me to do y' chips an' egg?" An' they're made up then. Bein' a part of it here, a proper part of it, it's much better than bein' on holiday.

She moves to the table and puts up the parasol

I have most of the days to meself an' just work the nights. I've got the night off tonight though. Well, Joe's arrivin' tonight. The first time he phoned, y' know after Jane had got back, he screamed at me. He said I must have finally gone mad. He said I was a disgrace — to the kids, to him, to meself. It was the easiest thing in the world to just put the phone down on him. The second time he phoned he said you can't run away from life. I said I agreed with him an' now I'd found some life I had no intention of runnin' away from it. He started to scream an' shout again. Then he said he knew all about me "holiday romance", an' how I'd made a fool of meself but — but if I stopped all this arsin' round, if I got meself on a plane an' got meself home, where I belonged, he said, he said he'd promise never to mention it. I said — said ... "The only holiday romance I've had is with meself, Joe. An' — an' I think ... I've come to like meself, really." I said to him, I said, "I think I'm all right, Joe. I think that if — if I saw me, I'd say that woman's OK ... She's alive. She's not remarkable, she's not gonna — gonna be there in the history books. But she's — she's there in the time she's livin' in. An' certainly she's got her wounds ... and her battle-scars but maybe — maybe ... a little bit of the bull-shit is true an' — an' the wounds shouldn't be hidden away ... because — because even the wounds an' the scars are about bein' alive." There was a long pause. I thought he'd gone off the phone. An' then I heard this voice, "I knew it," he was sayin', "I knew it, it's the bleedin' change of life, isn't it?" "That's right, Joe," I said, "that's right, it's a change of life. An'

that's why you're wastin' your money phonin' me to try an' get me back. I'm
not comin' back." The last time he phoned he said our Brian had been arrested
— buskin' without a licence. An' our Millandra was frettin' for me. An' that he
loved me an' the only thing he wanted in the world was for me to come back.
I explained to him that it was impossible because the woman he wanted to go
back didn't exist anymore. An' then I got his letter sayin' he was comin' to get
me. To take me back home. Ah, God love him, he must've been watchin'
Rambo. He'll be here soon. I hope he stays for a while. He needs a holiday. He
needs to feel the sun on his skin an' to be in water that's as deep as forever, an'
to have his wet head kissed. He needs to stare out to sea. And to understand.

Pause

I asked Costas if he'd put the table out for me again. He said to me,"You look
for you dream again?" "No, Costas," I said. "No dream. But I'm gonna sit here
an' watch for Joe an' as he walks down the esplanade, an' keeps walkin' because
he doesn't recognize me anymore, I'll call out to him. An' as he walks back, an'
looks at me, all puzzled and quizzical, I'll say to him, "Hello. I used to be the
mother. I used to be your wife. But now, I'm Shirley Valentine again. Would
you like to join me for a drink?"

Black-out

CURTAIN